St. Anne's Reel

St. Anne's Reel

Gil Garratt

St. Anne's Reel
first published 2015 by
Scirocco Drama
An imprint of J. Gordon Shillingford Publishing Inc.

Scirocco Drama Editor: Glenda MacFarlane
Cover design by Terry Gallagher/Doowah Design Inc.
Author photo by Trish Lindstrom
Printed and bound in Canada on 100% post-consumer recycled paper.

We acknowledge the financial support of the Manitoba Arts Council and The Canada Council for the Arts for our publishing program.

Library and Archives Canada Cataloguing in Publication

Garratt, Gil, author
St. Anne''s reel / Gil Garratt.

A play.
ISBN 978-1-927922-12-5 (pbk.)

I. Title.

PS8613.A784S83 2015 C812'.6 C2015-902526-5

J. Gordon Shillingford Publishing
P.O. Box 86, RPO Corydon Avenue, Winnipeg, MB Canada R3M 3S3

In memory of
Ernie King
(1930-2012)

Setting

A farm house kitchen.

Characters

WALTER, late 70s

DANIEL, late 30s

ANNE, a spectre

Notes on Staging

The tunes and music indicated are intended to reflect and support the characters and dramatic action of the play, and should be cut, vamped, stung, wrenched, excerpted and edited to fit this purpose. The tunes occur as part of the dramatic action, played with clear intentions; these are not 'show-tunes', or 'musical numbers' , but rather tactics used by these men to relate, alienate, comfort or attack each other.

Also, the spectre needn't be limited to the stage directions presented, with the caution to be spare: even the slightest movement and presence of such a silent character speaks volumes.

Production History

St. Anne's Reel was originally commissioned by the Blyth Festival and produced as part of its repertory season in the summer of 2014 with the following cast:

WALTER .... David Fox
DANIEL .... J.D. Nicholsen
ANNE .... Emily Lukasik

Directed by Marion deVries

Set and Costume Design by Joanna Yu

Lighting Design by Steve Lucas

Music Support by David Archibald and Anne Lederman

Stage Manager: Dustyn Wales

Apprentice Stage Manager: Georgia Priestley-Brown

Recorded voice of Young Danny: Gideon Garratt, age 8

On the Music

While this play is ostensibly steeped in a world of old time music, the actual necessities of performance in no way demand virtuosity. In the original cast, the role of Walter was played by a man in his seventies who had never played violin in his life and picked up the necessary rudiments for the role. The actor playing the spectre of Anne needs to be a competent fiddler, but the tunes themselves are actually quite basic depending on the arrangements; these are old time fiddle standards. The actor playing Daniel needs to be a proficient accompanist, but need not be accomplished. All of the tunes are traditional, and in the public domain.

Additionally: the song *Down Among the Budded Roses* is credited to Charlie Poole and is also in the public domain.

The Ranch Boys were a real house band for CKNX radio out of Wingham, Ontario, from 1935-1978.

Playwright's Notes

I arrived in Blyth, Ontario, for the first time, in August of 1999. The soy fields were just beginning to yellow, and the Cherrey Bus line still had a stop in town, in front of the General Store.

In the years since, I haven't passed a summer without looking over its fields or sitting in Blyth Memorial Hall at some point.

For a time, I owned a house in that town. My eldest son was born in that house. I planted cherry trees in the backyard there; they were just rooted twigs when I first put them in the soil; by the time I left, their fruit had filled jam jars.

Like so many of the people in that part of the world, I too have been pulled out of the ditch by a forgiving tractor on a foolish ice packed sideroad. At least once.

I have both eaten at church suppers and been on dishwashing duty.

And I have tried not to embarrass myself frantically playing my first banjo, in a patient circle of old time musicians, under a camper awning, in an unfinished basement, in a garage on the edge of town, singing over the smell of motor oil.

When I lived there, I did a lot of things, but the one thing I wish I'd done more of was listen.

Thomas Wolfe famously said "You can't go home again" and it has been held as a truism ever since. But to be honest (which is sometimes the hardest thing to be) I think Wolfe was only half right: It's true, you can't go home again. But you also can't ever really leave.

Gil Garratt

Gil Garratt is a playwright, director, dramaturge, Dora award-winning actor, and theatre administrator who has worked across Canada and internationally. With a career that has been dedicated primarily to the development of new plays, Gil is currently Artistic Director of the Blyth Festival, one of Canada's premier houses for new work. Gil is the founding Artistic Director of his own new performance development company: Clawhammer, dedicated to creating and producing innovative, interdisciplinary performance. Several of Gil's plays have received multiple productions, toured internationally, and been translated into French. He is a graduate of the National Theatre School's Playwriting Program.

Act I

Lights up slowly on an old man alone in a worn and ragged chair, in a dim, decrepit room, with fake wood paneling and décor that was dated and kitschy even when it was first applied some substantial time ago. Dishes are piled by the sink; beer bottles litter the room, as do clothes, tea towels, and local newspapers. The cupboards are bare, save for an omnipresent box of Carnation Instant Breakfast beside cans of evaporated milk.

The old man, WALTER, has a face that is creviced and craggy, like tanned elk hide. He is tall and physically imposing. He is dressed presentably, but in worn work pants, boots, an undershirt, and a dress shirt on top, half buttoned. His hair is sparse and white, but still carefully greased and combed in a style he has carried from his youth. He sits drinking a beer.

There are conspicuous vases of memorial flowers among the rubble.

As far from him as possible, but in a direct eye line, is a new violin case, on a small table.

Decision. Long walk across a silent house.

He touches the case for a long while. Opens the case. Takes out a fiddle and bow. Sits.

He takes in the fiddle. He rosins the bow. He breathes.

He starts to play, making several false starts. Another series of false starts. Finally he settles into the "Westphalia Waltz". WALTER's playing is strained, brutal and awkward, a once great fiddler who has had a recent stroke (about 18 months ago). WALTER can't complete the waltz, tries. Quits. Tries. He is obviously frustrated. He rests the fiddle resentfully on his lap.

A beautiful woman in a simple homemade wedding dress enters, her long hair is dripping wet. She crosses the stage unseen by WALTER. She too is holding a fiddle and a bow. This is ANNE. As she once was.

The woman stands behind WALTER's chair and raises her fiddle. WALTER, for all intents unaware of her presence, raises his fiddle again. As he starts the waltz anew, ANNE joins him, and while his playing is choked and strained, she plays the simple tune beautifully, such that his playing appears to magically improve and become fluid again.

DANIEL enters.

He sports a worn suede western jacket, threadbare jeans, battered cowboy boots. He carries a broken down guitar case and a battered canvas duffle bag.

DANIEL stands at the screen door, a long time, watching his father play, listening to the music. ANNE brings the tune to a close; as she stops, WALTER's own ragged playing trails out.

DANIEL: *Westphalia Waltz.*

Long silence. WALTER takes in DANIEL.

WALTER: How long you been standing there?

DANIEL: Long enough.

WALTER: How long?

DANIEL: Long enough to hear you playin' that Westphalia Waltz—

WALTER: Don't you figure I know what I'm playin'?

DANIEL: Look I didn't mean—

WALTER: What makes you think I need you telling me what the hell it is I'm playing?

DANIEL: I just heard you playing.

WALTER: Some nerve.

DANIEL: She taught me that one. She taught it to me, when I was…I heard you playin' it as I walked up. I couldn't believe…I thought…she, she taught it to me…I was just a kid, hardly hold the bow right. I'd grab it in my fist, all white knuckles. And she'd tell me to ease up, ease up Danny, she'd—

WALTER: That's far enough.

DANIEL: Pardon me?

WALTER: That's far enough.

DANIEL: Far. I. Look—I've been on the road a long time—

WALTER: What difference that make?

DANIEL: Well, I'd like to set these bags down.

WALTER: You think you're staying here do you?

DANIEL: Uh. Yeah to be honest I thought I might yeah.

WALTER: I don't think so.

DANIEL: And this is how it starts huh?

WALTER: How what starts?

DANIEL: I'm not in town, what, a couple hours, and already you're starting in on me.

WALTER: Oh, is that what I'm doing? Oh I see. You think, I'm just here starting in on you.

DANIEL: You know you are.

WALTER: Been sitting here all afternoon, waiting to start in on you. Just been here, burning a hole in this chair, waiting for you to get here so I could 'start in' on you.

ANNE exits.

DANIEL: Dad—

WALTER: You think that's what I been waiting for…burning a hole in this chair all day waiting for a chance to start in on you?

DANIEL: Please Dad.

WALTER: 'Please Dad'. Pleading in with 'Please Dad'.

DANIEL drops his stuff and steps further into the room.

Don't drop your stuff there.

DANIEL: What.

WALTER: I said don't drop your stuff there.

DANIEL: I heard you. Where do you want me to put it?

WALTER: You're not staying here.

DANIEL: Not staying here.

WALTER: That's what I said.

DANIEL: Fine. I'll find somewhere else.

WALTER: Then don't drop your stuff—

DANIEL: I'm not staying. I'm just putting it down alright. OK.

WALTER: Don't think you'll find it easy to find somewheres else. You don't know anyone around here anymore.

DANIEL: Well, that's my problem.

WALTER: Yes sir it is.

DANIEL: That's what I just said.

WALTER: I heard it.

Beat.

DANIEL: Can I have a drink? OK? Can I at least have a drink?

WALTER: There's water in the tap. You can wash your own glass. Don't touch my beer.

DANIEL: I'm not gunna touch your beer.

WALTER: Don't they drink Export down in Nashville? Don't they got Molson Export down in Nashville?

DANIEL: I don't want your beer.

WALTER: Too good for Export now are ya.

DANIEL: I just got my six month chip. OK. Six months clean and sober. I just got my six month chip for God's sake. I'm not gunna touch your beer.

WALTER: You are still in Nashville right? Haven't heard. Wasn't sure. Thought maybe you moved right into Dollywood or something.

DANIEL: I'm not living in. Nobody lives in Dollywood. It's an amusement park.

WALTER: No huh? So Nashville still then?

DANIEL: I'm between places.

WALTER: "Between places" that what they call being a hobo now?

DANIEL: Why the hell am I putting up with this?

WALTER: Oh well. Didn't you see that red carpet I rolled out out there? The ticker tape.

DANIEL: I didn't expect—

WALTER: Well what did you expect? What did you expect exactly?

DANIEL: I don't know.

WALTER: No c'mon, I wanna know. I wanna know what you expected. You show up here. After she has been laid in a box. Laid in a box.

DANIEL: Yes.

WALTER: Well I want to know what you expected.

DANIEL: Nothing's changed.

WALTER: Is that right? Seems to me a hell of a lot has changed. Your mother being dead for starters. Big change.

WALTER tries to fiddle but his playing is choked. DANIEL sits somewhere with his glass of water. In order to find a seat he must part rubble and wreckage. ANNE passes through the windows, with a handful of wildflowers. DANIEL looks to the bouquets on the table, cupboards. Again, ANNE is unseen by the men.

DANIEL: Helluva pile of flowers. Ya know, I've never really understood it, flowers. I mean sure, they're pretty. I get that. But they sure don't last. Wilt. Shrivel. Somebody comes to the door all full of outreach and condolences and they hand you flowers. And then they leave. And you're alone again. Alone in the house with the flowers, and they start, right then, to shrink and shrivel. The stems mould and rot, and the water goes brown, starts to stink. And you gotta take each vase full of rot and filthy water and throw it out. Death all over again.

WALTER: You still here?

DANIEL: I'm not going anywhere.

WALTER: I told you, you can't stay here.

DANIEL: I went by the funeral home. They want us there for seven-thirty. The visitation. They said you told them only one night.

WALTER: Not paying for two nights. They'll be cheek to jowl as it is. The UCW, Euchre Ladies, Cloggers, Choir, the whole damn Happy Gang. Wrinkled cheek to wizzled jowl.

DANIEL: Maybe we should do another night.

WALTER: No way. All in on the same night. If they want to come, if it's so important to them, they can cram their way in tonight. Two nights, there'd just be twice as many of them cramming in. Never get out of the place as it is.

DANIEL: She was a busy lady.

WALTER: Is that what she was?

DANIEL: Listen, can't we at least try to get along tonight. That's all I'm asking for.

WALTER: Seems to me you decided a long time ago that you were best to get along without me, or your mother.

DANIEL: You haven't let up since I walked in that door. We both know how long I been gone, and how soon I'm leaving again. So can't we just grit our teeth—

WALTER: Here I thought I was just going to fiddle some here

in my own home while the undertaker paints my wife's face in some cold basement somewhere and then who comes knockin'? Thought I'd just fiddle away the afternoon while they fill my wife's veins with formaldehyde.

DANIEL: Dad.

WALTER: But no, no. Hisself comes knockin'. Hisself. Well. Forgive me for not slaughtering the fatted calf, but I don't care for veal. Gives me gas.

Silence.

DANIEL: They told me you haven't been in since they picked her up.

WALTER: So.

DANIEL: They said you haven't been in at all. Not once. That you missed the family viewing this afternoon.

ANNE walks to WALTER.

WALTER: I told them I wasn't paying for that.

DANIEL: For fucksakes.

WALTER: I'm her only surviving family.

DANIEL: Are you.

WALTER: Well you been in already so what more do they want?

DANIEL: You haven't even been in to see her.

WALTER: I'm sure she doesn't mind.

DANIEL: You should go.

WALTER: Don't you go tellin' me what I should be doin'.

WALTER carves his way into a tune, possibly

"Rubber Dolly". As WALTER tries to play, ANNE joins him and takes it for him.

DANIEL looks away until WALTER abruptly stops.

DANIEL: What fiddle is that?

WALTER: It's new.

DANIEL: New. Yours?

WALTER: Hell yes it's mine.

DANIEL: Where'd you get it?

WALTER: Wingham.

DANIEL: Ernie?

WALTER: Yeah course it's Ernie. Know any other fiddle makers in Wingham?

DANIEL: Well I didn't assume you bought it new.

WALTER: Figured I picked it up at a flea market?

DANIEL: Why not?

WALTER: Flea market.

DANIEL: What's wrong with a flea market fiddle? You always told me—

WALTER: Don't think I deserve a new one?

DANIEL: Didn't say that.

ANNE exits upset.

WALTER: Don't think I deserve something custom made.

DANIEL: That's not what I'm saying.

WALTER: Oh I may not play the lunch time show in Dollywood—

DANIEL: Don't—

WALTER: I may not be some high-class hobo sleeping in the streets of Nashville—

DANIEL: Oh come on.

WALTER: I may not be high and mighty as hisself, but I earned me a new fiddle alright. I sure as hell earned it. Never had a new thing in my damn life, used cars, used tractors, Sally Ann clothes. Scrimped every dime to feed you, put clothes on your back.

DANIEL: I know you did.

WALTER: I sure as hell earned myself a brand new, brand new fiddle. For once.

DANIEL: I just meant to say—

WALTER: Did I ask for your opinion?

DANIEL: Nope. Volunteered it.

WALTER: Well I don't want it. Don't care for it.

DANIEL: That's fine.

WALTER: Sure is.

Beat.

DANIEL: What'd you do with your old one, your old fiddle.

WALTER: It's uh. I put it away.

DANIEL: The one Grandpa made for you?

WALTER: No he didn't make it.

DANIEL: I thought he made it.

WALTER: He repaired it. Worst deal of his life. Fella couldn't pay him for the work he done so he give him that fiddle. In pieces. Box full of broken fiddle pieces.

Your grandfather was just as stupid with his money as you are.

DANIEL: At least I come by it honestly. What happened to Mom's fiddle?

WALTER: She stopped playing it when she took sick. Had it on the wall above her bed, but she said she couldn't stand to look at it anymore, hanging like that, out of her reach. So I put it away for her. Just made her cry.

DANIEL: She couldn't play anymore?

WALTER: Not a note.

DANIEL: That's awful hard.

WALTER: Only got harder.

Beat. DANIEL's attention returns to the new fiddle.

DANIEL: What's Ernie done with the inlay there?

WALTER shows him.

DANIEL: Barndance. That's the old Barndance sign. Circle 8 Ranch. He did all that?

WALTER: Yep.

DANIEL: The Ranch Boys. Mother of pearl. It's gorgeous.

WALTER: Got my name on the back too.

DANIEL: Yeah. Wow.

WALTER: *(Reading from the inlay)* "Barndance and the Circle 8". Ranch Boys played both. "1949": year I started playing with them. "1978": year the station dropped us. Stopped broadcasting local music.

DANIEL: Huh.

WALTER: Yeah. Hell. Dropped us like a hot rock. They hardly even play country music on the AM station anymore. Nobody wants to hear old time music anymore. Oh, except the seniors dancing in the arena on Tuesday afternoons. It's all as good as dead. Used to be someone in every household in the county could play an instrument, now most of them can only play a radio. Just like that, it's gone.

DANIEL: God, Ernie's good.

WALTER: Last of his kind. Won't be another.

DANIEL: No up-and-comers in his shop?

WALTER: Oh, lots of 'em come and all of them go. Figure out there's no money in it.

DANIEL: Ah.

WALTER: So they quit.

DANIEL: Right.

WALTER: Everybody thinks you gotta make money. Like the money's what makes it worthwhile.

DANIEL: Too bad. That's too bad.

WALTER: It's a shame is what it is. A crying bloody shame.

Beat.

DANIEL: How's Ernie doing?

WALTER: Still doing his own roofing at 82.

DANIEL: Huh.

WALTER: Stopped singing though. Says the hearing aids make everything sound like a radio underwater in the middle of his head.

DANIEL: Your playing is good. You sound good.

WALTER: You're full of shit.

DANIEL: I'm just. I haven't heard you play in a long time. It sounds good.

WALTER: Bullshit. Bull. Shit. Don't you stand there and blow that sunshine bullshit up my—

DANIEL: When I walked up the lane I could hear you over the crickets out there, and I just stopped and listened for a bit. *(Beat.) Westphalia Waltz*. You played that for her on your wedding night.

WALTER: She told you that?

DANIEL: Yeah she told me. She told me Grandad held the reception out on the home farm, and you two snuck off, left everyone dancing in Grandad's driveshed with the cider pouring and the band…and you ran, into the front field. She said you stood all alone out there, and played her that tune. Hard dry sheaves of wheat on the ground, stars above. She danced and you played. She told me that when she folded her wedding dress into the old cedar chest in the attic, she wrapped a single piece of that dry ready grain between the silk folds. She told it to me when she taught me that one. I never forgot it. Tune or the story.

WALTER: Stroke.

DANIEL: What?

WALTER: Stroke. I had a damn stroke.

DANIEL: A stroke what? When?

WALTER: Over a year ago. Christmas. I can't hardly feel past the knuckles in my hands no more. Just crush the strings and Hail Mary and hope to hell something comes out.

DANIEL: Why didn't you call me?

WALTER: Why the hell didn't you call me?

DANIEL: Mom said nothing.

WALTER: Didn't need yer help then don't need it now.

DANIEL: You should have—

WALTER: Don't you go tellin' me what I should be doing.

DANIEL: I'm not tryin' to dammit.

WALTER tries to fiddle.

WALTER: Nothing I can't handle.

WALTER defiantly tries to start into "The Girl I Left Behind Me". ANNE helps him. WALTER's playing is crushed and weak, part way in DANIEL takes his guitar out of the case, he tries to help finish the tune.

DANIEL: That's the girl.

WALTER: *Girl I Left Behind Me.*

DANIEL: *Girl I Left Behind Me.* She never taught me to fiddle on that one. Didn't ever learn it.

WALTER: Nope. You didn't.

DANIEL: Still time. Still could.

WALTER: Could you. Bet you don't even have a fiddle anymore.

DANIEL: Maybe not.

WALTER: Probably hocked it.

DANIEL: Probably did.

WALTER: Your grandfather found that fiddle too.

DANIEL: I know.

WALTER: Repaired it. Too. Built it back up.

DANIEL: I know.

WALTER: And you, what, hocked it in some Tennessee pawn shop.

DANIEL: I did a lot of stupid things. Don't deny it.

WALTER: That was the fiddle she taught you on. Bigger than you when you started.

DANIEL: Yeah, I know that.

WALTER: And you sold it for what exactly?

DANIEL: I don't honestly remember. That's the sad truth. And I'm sorry I did it.

WALTER: You should be.

DANIEL: Nobody regrets it more than me. I'm just saying I could still learn it. Still learn that tune.

WALTER: Doubt there's anybody down there in Dollywood could teach you that one.

DANIEL: Lay off the Dollywood.

WALTER: Doubt there's anyone even in Nashville could.

DANIEL: I bet there is.

WALTER: Not the way I play it. Not the way she played it. Not the way it's played around here.

DANIEL: You don't know. Couple nights ago, right before I came out here, I got snuck in the back door to see Charley Pride play the Opry. Charley Pride. Still going strong. Right in the middle of his set, stripped down, no band, just Charley Pride and his guitar: (*Sung.*)"Kiss An Angel Good Morning, and love her like the devil when you get back home". The whole Opry on its feet. Old timers that have played with him for years, heard those songs a thousand times, and still they're standing and cheering for him. Hell of a show.

WALTER: Uh huh.

DANIEL: Nashville is just a... You can't see something like that anywhere else. Nowhere else.

WALTER: You can see that anywhere.

DANIEL: No you can't.

WALTER: Hell you could see Charley Pride in any major city in North America. See him in Toronto for godsakes. Watch him headline the CNE.

DANIEL: Not the same.

WALTER: Oh hell it is the same. The exact same set in every city. Same canned tracks.

DANIEL: They're not canned.

WALTER: Might as well be. You know well as I do that Charley Pride hasn't put out a decent record since 1977.

DANIEL: Thought you loved old music.

WALTER: That ain't old. That's just stale, like yesterday's donuts.

DANIEL: Well he's on the Opry again.

WALTER: And that's supposed to mean something to me?

DANIEL: The Opry dad. The Opry.

WALTER: What's that to me?

DANIEL: It's the Grand Ole Opry—

WALTER: You keep saying that like it should mean something.

DANIEL: Oh c'mon now. Anybody, anybody who—

WALTER: Hucksters. Hucksters selling generic snake oil.

DANIEL: You don't know what you're talking about.

WALTER: The Nashville Sound.

DANIEL: 4000 people clamour in there every night. Come from all over the world.

WALTER: Like a meat grinder: go in pasture fed prime rib come out sawdust hamburger.

DANIEL: What skin is it off your ass?

WALTER: You really don't get it.

DANIEL: Oh I get it. You've been sitting here fiddling since before the roads were paved, since before anybody had indoor plumbing. Just cause you never left this place doesn't make you a saint or something.

WALTER: Oh I gave up on sainthood some time ago.

DANIEL: By the time I came up there was no Barndance. No Circle 8 Ranch. There was nowhere for me to go here.

WALTER: You didn't even stay round here long enough to know there was nowhere for you.

DANIEL: My earliest memories are of crawling from my bed in the middle of the night and pressing my face, right there, between the loose rungs on the banister and listening to you and the Ranch Boys fill the midnight kitchen with Old Time Country Music. Air in here thick with blue smoke, and dirty jokes. And Mom'd tell me, get back up those stairs young man, but she'd be laughing as she said it. And she'd sit me on her knee, her fiddle on shoulder and we'd go.

And when I got older youse'd bring me down to sit with you at that arborite table; weekends, school nights, didn't matter. And I would play so hard to keep up. I'd bust my ass at that table, and I'd sleep through my classes the next day. I didn't care. I was gunna be a Ranch Boy myself one day. Play my own show on the CKNX. "From Coast to Coast, people love Country Music Most: It's the Saturday Night Barndance."

But then it was gone. End of story. Dead. There is nobody around here anymore who wants to pay a guy enough to put a roof over his head and food on his table for playing a bunch of old country songs. Oh, you could play once a month for the dinner crowd at the Candlelight, but you're never gunna make a living.

Look. Not everybody can find what they're looking for here.

WALTER: Oh, and you found what you were looking for down there.

DANIEL: I belong down there.

WALTER: That why you're 'between places'?

DANIEL: I needed a change alright.

WALTER: Change. Oh I see.

DANIEL: It's good for you. You should try it sometime.

WALTER: Oh well, I've got about as much change as I can handle at the moment thank you very much.

DANIEL: I didn't mean—

WALTER: Doesn't matter what you meant.

Beat.

DANIEL: I figured, the whole ride here. I figured. I walked through it. Outside Dayton, Interstate 71, I briefly thought you'd be happy to see me. By I75, I envisioned you with a shotgun chasing me down the road. By the time I hit Ontario though I knew, I knew it would be nothing as grandiose. Nothing as enormous as that. Just the same old sensation: being viciously gnawed on by a toothless dog. Locked on, but no real bite.

WALTER: Didn't ask you to come here.

DANIEL: Didn't ya? Jesus. You called me. You-Jesus-You.

WALTER: Did not call you.

DANIEL: Yes you did.

WALTER: No. No, I didn't call you. I tried. I tried to. But didn't even have no phone number for you. Lookit, your mother died and I thought, I thought somebody should tell you. I thought somebody—and I was willing to. After all this time I still thought… So I called the number in her book, disconnected. Then I called the only goddamn number— The only goddamn number I could think of. Called yer friggin' Dollywood. Even they didn't know where you were, they had no number, no forwarding address. But they said they'd look. So I left it at that. No other way to find you. But I sure as hell didn't call asking you to come here. You did that yerself. Your choice.

Beat

DANIEL: Was the cops told me in the end. A knock on the motel door. I was pretty scared at first. I knew it was bad. Nothing good comes of a couple of cops knocking on your motel door in the morning. One stood in the doorway, young one, never even stepped in the room. The other takes off his hat, bald head, sits on the edge of the unmade bed, and offers me coffee in a styrofoam cup. Keeps calling me Mr.Greaves. 'You see Mr.Greaves we had a call' I say, oh no, Mr.Greaves is my father, call me Dan. Said they had 'bad news from Canada'. 'Bad news from Canada, Dan'. Know what I figured? Figured you were dead. You. Figured it was *you*. Didn't even think it could be her. Didn't even. Not for a second. Didn't occur to me.

WALTER: Knew she was sick.

DANIEL: Not like that.

WALTER: She told you she was sick.

DANIEL: Not like that.

WALTER: When's the last time you talked to her?

DANIEL: Couple weeks? She told me she was feeling good. Strong.

WALTER: Things took a turn.

Stillness. WALTER surveys the field. ANNE crosses in the distance, possibly playing a slow, minor rendition of "St. Anne's Reel". Silence.

DANIEL: Can we just start this over?

WALTER: Start over.

DANIEL: Yeah. OK? Truce?

Beat. Both men look into the distance.

WALTER: So you're not back playing in Dollywood then, I take it.

DANIEL: I'm not talking Dollywood with you.

WALTER: Fine. *(Pause.)* You give up your Kris Kristofferson act finally.

DANIEL: What Kristofferson act?

WALTER: All that, the, all the crap the songwriting you were. You were writing songs.

DANIEL: I thought I was a songwriter. Yes.

WALTER: So you give up that up now, didja?

DANIEL: I don't want to talk about that either.

WALTER: Well.

Silence.

DANIEL: Cornfields look good.

WALTER: Do they. *(Beat.)* Yes. Suppose they do. Still on the field though.

DANIEL: Right.

WALTER: Can't count your crop in the field.

DANIEL: Contracted?

WALTER: Nope. Taking my chances.

DANIEL: When you taking it off?

WALTER: When I get a chance. Been kind of busy, you see.

Beat

Three cuts of hay though.

DANIEL: Three.

WALTER: Yeah.

DANIEL: That's good.

WALTER: Sure as hell is.

DANIEL: Thought maybe you'd be renting the fields out.

WALTER: Don't think I can hack it.

DANIEL: Not saying that.

WALTER: I can still drive that tractor.

DANIEL: Don't doubt it.

WALTER: And the Schultz boys are partnered up here now anyway.

DANIEL: Schultz boys. They still around, eh.

WALTER: Damn good farmers.

DANIEL: I bet they are.

WALTER: Damn good farmers.

Beat. DANIEL doesn't take the bait.

Didn't hear your car in the lane. What are you driving these days?

DANIEL: Greyhound.

WALTER: Greyhound?

DANIEL: I took the bus here.

WALTER: Is that right?

DANIEL: It was fine. Poured rain outside Cincinnati. Clear otherwise.

WALTER: Nice view from the window seat?

DANIEL: It was just fine.

WALTER: You're on the wagon then?

DANIEL: Yes. I am.

WALTER: Six months.

DANIEL: Yeah, six months.

WALTER: Six months.

DANIEL: That's what I said.

WALTER: I've had heartburn that lasted longer than—

DANIEL: —/ I bet you have /—

WALTER: —/ Six months.

WALTER picks at the fiddle on his lap.

DANIEL: You know, the point isn't the six months.

WALTER: Oh isn't it.

DANIEL: It takes a hell of a lot longer than six months to get that chip. It takes a lot longer. Took me a lot longer.

WALTER snorts.

DANIEL: Is it really so hard to be civil?

WALTER: I'm being civil.

DANIEL: You're impossible.

WALTER: Just not going to sit here and smile and play nice. It's bull. Forget it.

DANIEL: Then don't say anything.

WALTER: Sounds good to me.

DANIEL: Can't even have a conversation.

WALTER: Guess not.

DANIEL starts into something darker, minor, like "Cluck Old Hen". WALTER tries to add in, with ANNE joining him. There is a competitive edge to the duet/duel between WALTER and DANIEL. But WALTER stops abruptly, turns away, retreats. DANIEL sees. There is a lingering awkwardness when they finish. Silence.

DANIEL makes his way to reading some of the littered cards from sympathizers.

DANIEL: Helluva pile of cards. She's gunna be missed. Surprised the Legion Ladies haven't sent someone over to beg for her recipes. They been coming by a lot?

WALTER: Who now?

DANIEL: The service ladies. Dropping in on you a lot?

WALTER: Suppose.

DANIEL: They saying much? Good stories.

WALTER: Wouldn't know.

DANIEL: Wouldn't know?

WALTER: Wouldn't know.

DANIEL: Somebody must have brought all this. These flowers.

WALTER: Suppose somebody did.

DANIEL: Well?

WALTER: Don't have to talk to them.

DANIEL: What.

WALTER: Yeah, they been coming round. They don't stick around long.

DANIEL: You don't even talk to them.

WALTER: Come around here like lost kittens who can't find their saucer of milk. They mew and whine out there looking for it. Looking for her.

DANIEL: Honestly—

WALTER: That's who the flowers are for. Her.

DANIEL: You really believe that.

WALTER: They're not bringing them around for me. I don't have to talk to them. I am not obligated—

DANIEL: It's not an obligation.

WALTER: Sure as hell is. And there will be enough of it tonight. Every old biddy in the township will be dusting off her black hat and piling onto her neighbour's lap and coming by the sedan load.

DANIEL: That's supposed to be a good thing.

WALTER: Shake my hand like so many cold limp breakfast sausages. Wiping their eyes with the embroidered hanky they pressed just for the occasion.

DANIEL: It's grief. They're grieving—

WALTER: And I'll have to stand there. Stand there and look on, like their 'grief' is some kind of blessing on me.

DANIEL: They are paying their respects—

WALTER: Respects. I'll have to stand there and watch each one peer into Annie's waxed face and tell me how peaceful she looks. Peaceful. Of course she looks peaceful, her face is two thirds paraffin and half formaldehyde now… She looks like she's sleeping because her eyelids are glued shut and her lips are sewn…that dress, pinned and pressed and hot glued in place on her cold skin. Sagging off her still. Married in that dress.

DANIEL: Her wedding dress.

WALTER: What you want me to bury her in, a potato sack?

DANIEL: No, just—

WALTER: Not my idea in the first place. Undertaker's. And every one of those old biddies is gunna be looking close enough to see the moth holes and water stains, and they won't say it to my face, but at their bridge game, or their next bloody church dinner, they'll whisper it, whisper what a shame it was, how shameful it was. Sip their tomato juice and pretend to be civilized and all the while hissing on about the shame it was.

DANIEL: They're not gunna do that.

WALTER: You got no idea. No idea.

DANIEL: They just care. They come cause they care. They bring flowers cause they care.

WALTER: They might as well be throwing them directly on the manure pile. Don't even bother ringing the bell. Just walk around back and toss them. Couldn't care less. And give those bone dry banana muffins directly to the dog. I should make a sign. I should make a sign. Put a sign out there to that effect. Thanks for coming. Please pitch your flowers directly into the—

DANIEL: OK. You made your point.

WALTER: Oh. Oh. I see. Didn't realize we were playing for points.

DANIEL: I don't think you know how to play any other way.

ANNE herself starts to play this time. WALTER, without conscious awareness is drawn in and joins her. DANIEL follows…something dueling, perhaps "Growling Old Man, Grumbling Old Woman". WALTER and DANIEL battle their way through a brief version with an abrupt stop, crash, by WALTER, who interrupts viciously with—

WALTER: You stop that now.

DANIEL: What.

WALTER: Don't you look at me like that.

DANIEL: I wasn't looking at you like anything.

WALTER: Hell you weren't.

DANIEL: It's almost seven. Is that what you're wearing?

WALTER: You been looking at me sideways since you come in that door.

DANIEL: We have to be there for seven-thirty.

WALTER: Do you think I don't know what I sound like?

DANIEL: Sorry.

WALTER: Don't you dare pity me. You really think you're something. Think I lost it all now do ya? Think you got something on me.

DANIEL: No. I don't.

WALTER: Toothless dog huh? Toothless dog.

DANIEL: Is that what you're wearing?

WALTER: Some nerve.

DANIEL: It's almost… OK. Fine. Can I borrow your iron?

WALTER: If you can find it.

DANIEL leaves the room. Cursing and banging offstage. DANIEL comes back with iron and ironing board. Eventually he starts on a crumpled shirt he has had in his guitar case. It is clear from his movements that DANIEL could count on one hand the garments he has ironed in his life. Though his suit is tasteful, it was likely at one time a costume he performed in, a fact not lost on WALTER. All of this action occurs under the continuing scene.

DANIEL: Are you going to change your clothes or not?

Beat.

If you've got a shirt I'm willing to press it for you.

WALTER: Mister Dollywood.

DANIEL: I told you to lay off the Dollywood. I got paid good money down there.

WALTER: Playing afternoon shows for the cotton candy crowd.

DANIEL: Good money.

WALTER: Right between the magic act and the puppet show.

DANIEL: I'm a working musician. It was a good gig.

WALTER: Powder blue suits like a bunch of cartoon cowboys.

DANIEL: I liked working there. OK.

WALTER: Cap gun six shooters in rhinestone holsters.

DANIEL: How would you know. You never even saw me.

WALTER: Spurs that jingle jangle jingle.

DANIEL: You don't know how hard I busted my— Six shows a day, six days a week.

WALTER: Oh you're hard workin' alright. Hard workin' "between places". A hard workin' hobo who won't come home until his mother's in a pine box.

DANIEL: Back off.

WALTER: Singing your heart out for those picture postcard family vacationers while your own mother was sick in bed, rolling in the cancer ward.

WALTER takes another beer from the fridge.

DANIEL: I'm not taking you to the funeral home drunk.

Beat.

WALTER: I'm not going to the funeral home.

DANIEL: What.

WALTER: I'm not going. I'm not gunna stand there through that procession of old biddies. I'm not going anywhere. You think that six month chip entitles you to something? You think that six month chip entitles you, entitles you to look down on me. Think it makes you more than me.

DANIEL: That is not what I think.

WALTER: Oh I know it does.

DANIEL: You don't know a thing.

WALTER: Six months.

DANIEL: Are you honestly not coming to her visitation?

WALTER: Six months.

DANIEL: Her visitation.

WALTER: Six months.

DANIEL: Your own wife. Your own—

WALTER: They don't want to see me. They just wanna see Annie. They just wanna see Saint Annie in her satin lined box. Spit their pity in my face.

DANIEL: Look, nobody is going to—

WALTER: Oh really. No. Think that. You think that. You go ahead and think that.

DANIEL: She is not even…she's not even cold in the ground and already you, already you are— They haven't even dug the hole where they're gunna drop her, and you already want to turn your back on her. But that's the way you work isn't it. Minute somebody leaves out that door you just close it behind them.

WALTER: I don't need you here. Haven't needed you here for a long time.

DANIEL: Yeah, I see that.

WALTER: Partnered up with the Schultz boys on the fields. Don't need you around here. *(Beat.)* She could have used you though. She could have.

DANIEL: What?

WALTER: She could have used you. Midnights, coughing blood, nobody here but me with my Molson Export bedside manner. She could have used you. But of course you were in Dollywood, and couldn't be here. Couldn't be home here. After the doctors wrung their hands and sent her home. But no. You'll come a couple days on a bus to shake hands with every mournful member of the UCW. The prodigal son.

And now you want to grandstand here and show me how you are the one knows how to mourn her right. Go damn it. Go play nice. Go play long lost broken hearted son. Go. Reformed and Redeemed.

For eighteen years. For eighteen years I have been sitting here telling her you're never coming back. That you would never come back. I told her that. Every Christmas. Every harvest. Every spring. Every wedding and funeral that went by. Eighteen years I told her you were never coming back.

I knew you wouldn't ever come back. I know you very well.

DANIEL is silent.

Even now. Right now. Looking at you. I can tell you exactly what's gunna happen for you next. I know. You are going to storm out of here. Soon. You can't take much more of the old man. You will kick over the ironing board on your way out...some futile retaliation. You are going to stand on the porch and resist weeping. Like a little boy. Pulling on your own hair. You'll want, so bad, to come back in here and fight your ground. To tell me off. But you won't. You won't. You'll figure: cut your losses. You are going to walk into town to go to the visitation. You will hitchhike in, and no one will pick you up. Gravel dust and mud on your spit shined shoes. You will stand outside the parlour and look at the people lined in the street and you will realize that they all know who you are. What. You. Are. And you will turn away, run into the closest field, running from the people who know you. And *you* will stand there in the summer night and you will cry. Like a baby. You will cry like a naked little baby. You are not here to remember your mother, to honour her; you are only here for yourself.

DANIEL explodes. He storms out of the house.

Silence.

DANIEL re-enters.

Gently and deliberately, looking his father steadily in the eye, DANIEL carefully kicks over the ironing board. Slowly exits.

ANNE looks at WALTER. WALTER sees ANNE.

ANNE, hurt, slowly exits. WALTER rushes to where he saw her. She is gone.

WALTER is alone.

End of Act I.

Act II

Pre-dawn hours that same night. Lights up to reveal WALTER still awake, alone in the house, sitting in his worn and ragged chair. Open on the table is an old reel-to-reel tape recorder. Beside it are small piles of open reels, and several full boxes. The tape is not playing. ANNE is out the screen door, watching the dark road.

DANIEL enters, staggering. He is covered in mud and blood. Shock. Concussed. WALTER shuts off the machine.

WALTER: What the hell happened to you?

DANIEL: They were all there… All of them.

WALTER: Who now?

DANIEL: I walked all the way in, my thumb out. Every car just passed me by.

WALTER: You look like—

DANIEL: All of them…every old face I ever knew. Staring at me like I was a ghost in the street. Jaws dropped. Gaping, gaping like, fish. Like a line of brook trout standing in the street. Gasping. Watching a ghost in the streetlight. They put in all those new lamp-posts downtown, new old lamp-posts…like old gas lamps. This town never had real gas lamps. But they put in those black, fake gas lamps, with no gas, like a pretend village, like a Christmas village in a store window. Pretend lamp posts. It's like—I don't know—they're putting a ribbon on everything, picturesque, like it's always been quaint here. As if we should believe those are real wagon wheels at the end of every lane. And they're looking at me, these lamp lit brook trout. Sick. I feel sick. I back away, back away all the way into the ball diamond, the lion's park, into the field and stand there…

WALTER: You got blood all over your face. Danny.

No response.

You got blood all over your face.

No response.

What—

DANIEL: Truck on the way home. I was walking on the gravel road. I heard him coming. I was on the shoulder, but he clipped me. Clipped me hard, I guess. Fast. Going fast.

WALTER: Blue Ford?

DANIEL: Didn't see.

WALTER: Bet it was Herb. Son of a. Drives like a maniac on that road. Blue Ford? *(WALTER goes to the freezer.)* Haven't got any ice… Bag of peas? You want a bag of peas? For your face? Peas?

DANIEL: He didn't stop.

WALTER: Who now?

DANIEL: Truck. Didn't stop.

WALTER: Course not.

DANIEL: Lying there. Couldn't get up.

WALTER: Probably figured he hit a deer.

DANIEL: Still should have stopped.

WALTER: Probably six sheets to the wind. Do you want these peas?

DANIEL: What are you listening to?

WALTER: Heh?

DANIEL: The reel-to-reel. What's on the tape?

WALTER: Nothing.

DANIEL: From the radio station?

WALTER: Yeah.

DANIEL: Barndance?

WALTER: Yeah, old Barndance. I says, do you want these peas?

DANIEL: Barndance. Old Barndance reel. Ranch Boys?

WALTER: Yeah Ranch Boys. Barndance. Here take these peas, dammit. You're all shook up. You. You should sit down.

DANIEL: There were a lot of folks there. At her visitation. They asked about you. They all asked about you.

WALTER: Thought you went to the ball diamond.

DANIEL: I did. I went to the field… Standing there. Alone. I felt. I felt drunk. Drunk. Been dry, completely dry six months. Got my six months and I feel drunk. The stars. I'd forgotten how they come out here. Closer. It's like the stars are all closer here.

I take a breath, a deep breath, and it feels like the first breath I have taken in, in years. And I walk back in there. Walk back in there and shake every hand. I hand out Kleenex. Take flowers. Thank them all for their flowers. Old ladies keep taking me by the arm and telling me how glad they are that I'm home. Home. Keep telling me how happy they are to have me home. How I look, how I look like her. They kept asking after you. Said they were gunna put us in their prayers. And then I left. And I got hit by a truck. Shit. I got hit by a truck.

WALTER: Here take these peas, wouldja.

DANIEL takes the peas, and almost immediately sets them back down as he goes to the sink and washes his hands and face. He slowly regains clarity. He sees WALTER's fiddle.

DANIEL: Ernie told me about the fiddle.

WALTER: What now.

DANIEL: Ernie told me. He was at the visitation. Told me about the fiddle you're playing. *(Beat.)* Why didn't you say so. *(Pause.)* Why didn't you just tell me. Why didn't you just tell me that?

WALTER: What difference does it make.

DANIEL: It makes a huge difference.

WALTER: it doesn't change anything.

DANIEL: Sold her…sold her wedding ring and… She was dying and she bought it for you. Custom made. Custom made. For you.

WALTER: Didn't ask her to. Did not ask her to do that.

DANIEL: You ungrateful— Won't even go to her visitation. God. How. This. This is exactly. You can't let anything in can you. Can't let anything affect you. All my life, all her life, Even as she's dying. She gives you a gift like that and you, you just stay stone cold.

WALTER: Are you finished?

DANIEL: No. No. I'm not. Standing in that field tonight. Standing there, before I manned up and walked back into that funeral parlour—where you sure as hell should have been—standing there, it come to me. I didn't leave here to get away from you. I left here because I didn't want to become you. Don't want to become you.

When I was a kid, and Mom would let me stay up late, sitting on the couch in my flannel pyjamas, so we could watch you. Watch you and the Ranch Boys, on the Circle 8, on that fifteen inch screen, with the rabbit ears taped in place. I'd see you on TV there and I would try to understand, watch you cracking jokes and sawing away, slaps on the back, and I'd think: what it would take for him to enjoy playing with me like that?

And I…worked blisters into my fingers all night every night out in that drive shed, under the propane heaters in the dead of winter, reaching after it for—for one reason. For you. For you. To be like you. Because I thought… But you. You just stayed stone cold.

DANIEL catches his breath. WALTER flicks on the reel to reel. He rewinds the section he listened to earlier. Hits play. ANNE and DANIEL's laughter comes over the speakers. In the recording ANNE is young and DANIEL is a child, eight years old. They are heard giggling and tuning instruments. The spectre of ANNE re-emerges throughout, her voice on the recording.

ANNE: Danny. What are you doooing? (Laughter.) Are you ready or what?

DANNY: Or what?

ANNE: C'mon you wise guy.

DANNY: I'm ready. I'm ready. Almost.

ANNE: *OK let's do it in D. D for dog.*

DANNY: *I know Mom.*

ANNE: *I'm just reminding you.*

DANNY: *OK. Ready.*

ANNE: *And a one, two, three*

Stumble. Laughter.

DANIEL: You said it was old Barndance reels. The Ranch Boys…

They listen.

DANNY: *OK OK start over. Start over.*

ANNE: *The tape is rolling here you know.*

DANNY: *Count me in again.*

DANIEL: You been listening to this all night? You been sitting here listening…

WALTER gently shushes DANIEL.

They listen.

ANNE: *And a one, two, three…*

DANNY & ANNE: *(Singing.) Little sweetheart we have parted*
from each other we must go
Many miles may separate us
in this world of care and woe

ANNE: *You take it now Danny.*

DANNY: *Down among the budded roses*
I am nothing but a stem
I have parted from my darling
never more to meet again

DANIEL: I didn't know these were still around.

WALTER: Both those boxes.

ANNE & DANNY: *But I treasure dear your promise*
that you'll meet me in the lane

DANIEL: They all her and me?

WALTER: Pretty much.

They listen.

ANNE & DANNY: *Where we'll always be together;*
when the roses bloom again
Now this parting gives me sorrow
and it almost breaks my heart
Tell me darling will you love me
when we meet no more to part

Fiddle and guitar break, Mother and Son.

DANIEL: We used to get out that old four-track every Sunday after we got home from church. She used to say the choir warmed her up. She'd. She'd teach me a tune every week, a new tune, and Sunday, on Sunday she'd get out the four-track and we'd try to do it. She called them our Mother and Son Sunday Sessions.

WALTER shuts off the machine.

WALTER: I used to give her hell about it. Wasting tape.

DANIEL: She kept them. All of them.

WALTER: More boxes in the attic. She used to listen to them, at night. Kept a box of her favourites under the bed. She'd do the dishes, or be folding laundry, or… Last few months usually she'd just sit right here. Sit and listen.

DANIEL: And this is what you've been doing tonight. Whole community is down at that funeral home, and you are sitting here alone listening to her sing in the dark?

WALTER: Used to be able to split and stack two full face cords in a day. When the creek was frozen solid, drag out the dead wood with that old red belly Ford. Chains so cold they'd sting your hands right through your gloves. When you were a kid you'd follow with your ice skates, and after the trees were dragged out the snow would be near clear off the ice and you'd get out there and pretend you were Phil Esposito, or Bobby Orr. Or somebody.

Summer time, when the day was good and dry, no engine calling to be overhauled, no jammed up blades on the baler to deal with, and I'd split. Stack. Two cords. Full cords. Two cords in a day. Always four years ahead. Always gotta stay four years ahead.

Nowadays I get the Schultz boys to give me a hand. Still drive the tractor, but they fell the trees. They split it. Humour me as I stack the top rows. Tarp it. I still carry it in all winter. Some years I'd rather just buy slab from the sawmill. But I get her done.

They run the gas line, natural gas line up this concession, forty years ago. Everybody switched over to gas furnaces. Not me. Pipefiiters, made a mess of the road all along here. Took months. Drove me crazy all that summer because the Ranch Boys we were on tour. We were playing live radio hook ups from fairs and town halls all over hell's half acre. Circle 8 Ranch every Tuesday night.

Most of that was me and Rossie on fiddle, Don on his guitar, Cora on accordion and keys, with Reg just trying to keep up with us. *(He laughs.)* The Ranch Boys. We were playing easy three hundred parties and dances a year in those days. We would get home to the radio station in the pitch dark and I'd drive out to the farm, and that summer the road was all torn up. Because of the gas line. Fields were a shamble of weeds. Was barely even a weekend farmer then.

I met your mother at a homecoming dance in Whitechurch. She was there in a homemade sky-blue dress, with a matching ribbon in her hair and a fiddle under her chin. She could hoot and holler with the best of them, better. She was like a firecracker disguised as a communion candle. Everyone around her lit up.

Your mother was only seventeen when we got married. She floated down that aisle like an angel among us. My Saint Anne. Everyone assumed she was pregnant. Her father glared at me with fireball eyes ablaze all through the service. But she wasn't. Didn't have you for more than ten years after that. Surprised them all.

After we were married I didn't like her coming with me to the dances, and parties, all the drinking and trouble around. Most of it harmless, but I was tight fisted with her. Tight fisted. Didn't like the way men watched her twirl in her homemade summer dresses. So I told her, I made her, stay home.

When the road was torn up, she was alone all the time. Pretty young town girl in a farm house by herself. Day and night. Summer heat. Day and night. She'd have trouble sleeping, so she'd go and swim in the creek in the dark. I'd come home and find her in bed at night with her hair wet.

I'd be gone after breakfast most days. Back out on the circuit.

She was all alone. Farm house. Alone. She started making lemonade, baking pies in the summer kitchen, walking them down to talk to the pipefitters. Laugh with the pipefitters. Toss her hair for the pipefitters.

I never knew his name. I found his Chevy flat bed in the laneway. Both of them with wet hair.

Silence.

I made sure they capped that gas line at the road, end of the lane, and I. I went on splitting wood. Two cords in a good day…

Somewhere during WALTER's story, ANNE might appear in the distant fields, hair dripping wet, walking toward the house.

This was years before you were born. Years before.

Silence.

DANIEL stands.

DANIEL: I don't want to stay here.

WALTER: Just sit back down.

DANIEL: *(He picks up his bag, and starts stripping off his funeral clothes and scrambling back into the clothes he arrived in.)* Every time. Every time I try to. Every time I try to reach out and grab onto something it just slips. It crumbles and slips right between my, my. I. Every single time. I thought. I somehow thought. I thought. Every thing. Every thing I want to lean on. I didn't. I didn't need to know that. You didn't have to tell me that.

WALTER: Sit down Daniel.

DANIEL: Why did you tell me that?

WALTER: I was trying to explain—

DANIEL: What? That you had the right to treat her…to not go to her visitation?

WALTER: No.

DANIEL: Because of some, because of some stupid thing happened forty years ago?

WALTER: Now that's not—

DANIEL: Why did you tell me she did that?

WALTER: I was trying to…

DANIEL: Why did you tell me she did that?

WALTER: I'm trying to show you…

DANIEL: Show me what?

WALTER: That she could do no wrong. No wrong by me. I. I. No matter. No matter. It's not even that I forgive her, it's that I understood, I understood what she needed, why she needed to…and I loved her all the same. Maybe more.

I spent that night alone, out in the front field. Beans yellowed all around my knees, thick with burdock and ragweed, choked and shrivelled with muck. I left it all alone too long. I was away too long. You can't leave things alone all the time. You just can't. That's when the weeds come in.

Long pause.

DANIEL: Please. Come with me to the funeral home. Come see her.

WALTER: No. I'm not. I'm not gunna. I'm not.

DANIEL: Dad—

WALTER: No Danny no. I can't. I don't want. I can't see her like that. Full of weeds.

I just wanna listen. Listen to her here.

Used to make me so mad when you'd waste the tapes.

Silence. WALTER turns the reel-to-reel back on. ANNE is heard fiddling, both in the recording and gently live. DANIEL reaches over and turns the volume down very low.

DANIEL: I used to call her on the phone whenever things got… And she would do this thing. She'd. She'd just start telling me about the peaches she'd picked up in town, or the church rummage sale, how the fish fry went, or what bulbs are coming up in the garden…and the whole world would slow down… Every time I called her she'd find a way to…

Most of that first year down in Nashville, I slept in the cab of that old El Camino, parked out on backroads outside of town. Abandoned parking lots. Didn't know anybody. Nobody knew me. Somehow I worked up the nerve to put my name on the list for an open mic night at the Bluebird Café in Green Hills. Sitting there in the crowd, watching act after act, listening for my name, I start to feel the sweat pooling in the back of my shirt. Hands trembling. My guts turning over and over like I'm in an elevator with the cables cut, falling straight down the shaft. I run out of the place, hand over my mouth like I'm gunna be sick.

Phone booth outside. I scramble into it. Beg the operator to place the call, and Mom comes on. Accepts the charges. And right away she hears the panic in my throat. Hears me gasping. And she just slowed it all down.

I walk back into the Bluebird in time to hear my name and I take the stage…and I bomb so hard, real hard…sound of one hand clapping… But I walked back in there. And I couldn't do it without her there, without her there to slow it down.

I— I. I remember. I remember this one summer, was just a kid…must have been end of June or early July, cause I remember my fingers were pink from eating all the wild raspberries by the old pig pens.

You had the baler in pieces down in the shade by the shed, oil rag in your hands. You were cursing some thing or other. I remember that. I remember keeping a wide berth.

I walk to the rope swing in the old butternut tree…

I get on that swing, and somehow I step right on a ground hornets' nest. D'you remember this?

Suddenly hundreds of hornets swarming me, stinging every inch… The buzzing roar in my ears, I close my eyes tight, swatting them from my face… they're everywhere…bite my lips, bite my eyelids, my hands, my…and I'm running, screaming for the house…but before I can make it to the door you're standing there. Face all red. You lift me with one hand, and start smacking them off me. You throw me in the shower, cold water, holding me under it, trying to get them all off me.

WALTER: Friggin' hornets.

DANIEL: You wrap me in a towel, and tell me to rub butter on my welts, to pull the stingers out if I see any. And you go back outside, and I watch from the window. You, storming toward the swing, carrying a jerry can of gasoline. You pour it all over the ground where the hornets are still rising and you light it all on fire.

I remember watching you stand there, still, silent. Fire eating up the rope swing, devouring the ground, black smoke rising.

You were trying to protect me.

Long pause.

WALTER: Right there see. I can't hardly feel past the knuckles in these hands no more. Right in this hand, right here in this hand I used to hold them. I had them right here in this hand, hundreds and hundreds of tunes. Held them there effortless as a heart beat. Now I just crush the strings and Hail Mary and hope to hell something comes out.

I quit playing, after the stroke. Whole house went quiet, and she hated it. Asked me over and over to start again, to try again. But I couldn't. Hated it. Get so... But she'd keep asking. I took a hammer to that old fiddle your grampa made me, and burned the splinters in that stove. Just couldn't stand lookin at it. But she wouldn't let go. That's when she had this one made for me.

Your mother died in a quiet house and it was the last thing she ever wanted. She got this one made and, this, tonight, this is the first time I ever picked it up. Tonight. She never even got to hear it.

You're right Danny, it's like you said. They slip, things slip right through your fingers. Everything slipped.

WALTER exits.

DANIEL is alone.

ANNE appears silhouetted in the window.

WALTER returns, carrying an old, battered and repaired violin case.

WALTER: Now don't start arguing with me.

DANIEL: What?

WALTER: She'd want you to have it.

DANIEL doesn't take it.

WALTER: You said you sold the other one.

DANIEL doesn't take it.

You can't learn to play it right if you don't have one. A decent one. Just take the damn thing.

DANIEL: I haven't touched it in years. I don't remember. I don't remember…

WALTER: She'll help you Danny. She'll help you. She'll show you the way son. Here now, here. She'd want you to have it.

DANIEL opens the case, and takes out the fiddle.

ANNE with her fiddle. WALTER takes up his fiddle.

Give me your A.

DANIEL: What. My what?

WALTER: Give me your A. I need your A. I'll come to you.

DANIEL takes up his fiddle, plays his open A. WALTER and ANNE and DANIEL tune to each other easily. With ANNE's help, they reach for the "Westphalia Waltz".

Eventually ANNE stops and leaves the men to finish out the tune. Their playing should be predictably awful, terrible, scratchy, without artistry or grace… very poor. Both men know it. And for the first time they laugh, at themselves, in spite of themselves, and with each other.

Dawn creeps over the fields.

Exit ANNE, possibly playing "St. Anne's Reel".

The End.